London Underground Steam

Kevin McCormack

Ian Allan
PUBLISHING

Front cover: With office workers watching from their windows and smartly dressed LT station staff officiating, Class E 0-4-4 tank No L44 prepares to return to Neasden with the replica contractor's trucks and accompanying brake vans following the tableau presented to the Lord Mayor's party at Barbican station on 24 May 1963 as part of the Underground Centenary celebrations. *Roy Hobbs*

Back cover: A wreath adorns the smokebox of Ivatt Class 2MT 2-6-2 tank No 41284 as it heads for Chalfont & Latimer with the Met's late-Victorian push/pull-fitted carriages on the last day of steam operation on the Chesham branch, 11 September 1960. *Roy Hobbs*

Previous page: Ex-GWR '57xx' 0-6-0 pannier tank No L89, built at Swindon in 1929, shunts at Croxley Tip on 30 June 1969. Water splashes from overfilling the tank have revealed that this locomotive is not, after all, painted black! *David Clark*

First published 2011

ISBN 978 0 7110 3406 8

© Ian Allan Publishing Ltd 2011

Published by Ian Allan Publishing

an imprint of Ian Allan Publishing Ltd, Hersham, Surrey, KT12 4RG
Printed in England by Ian Allan Printing Ltd, Hersham, Surrey, KT12 4RG

Code: 1102/B1

Distributed in the United States of America and Canada by BookMasters Distribution Services

Visit the Ian Allan Publishing website at www.ianallanpublishing.com

Introduction

This colour album portrays steam operations on the London Underground from the mid-1950s through to withdrawal in 1971. The photographs cover the locomotives actually owned by the London Passenger Transport Board and its successors (henceforth referred to as 'LT') as well as those belonging to British Railways (BR) hauling LT passenger trains. In the period covered by this book LT's own locomotives were confined to freight/engineering trains and shunting, except when the handful of surviving Class E 0-4-4 tanks occasionally reprised their former passenger role by hauling railtours on the Underground. As regards BR-hauled LT passenger trains, these operated on the Central Line's Epping–Ongar service (until 1957), the Metropolitan Line's branch from Chalfont & Latimer to Chesham (until 1960) and the Rickmansworth–Aylesbury section of the Metropolitan's 'main line' from Baker Street (until 1961). The latter two services involved the use of LT stock.

For ease of reference the abbreviation 'Met' is used for the Metropolitan Railway and, after its absorption by LT in 1933, the Metropolitan Line. Similarly, the Metropolitan District Railway and its successor, the District Line, are both referred to as the 'District'.

The Met was the world's first underground railway and started running services between Paddington and Farringdon in 1863, using steam locomotives owned by the Great Western Railway (GWR). Ironically, the last steam engines owned by LT were former GWR locomotives, albeit purchased from BR. These created a standard fleet to replace the Met steam engines inherited by LT, which, by the mid-1950s, were becoming worn out and beyond economic repair (although some lasted until 1963) and also to replace the two relatively modern District locomotives. As, at this time, no suitable alternative motive power (electric or diesel) had been found, there remained a continuing requirement for steam until 1971 for certain freight/engineering trains.

As a result of a disagreement between the Met and the GWR, resulting in the latter's refusal to continue providing trains for the initial service and forcing the Met to borrow from the Great Northern Railway, the Met needed a fleet of its own locomotives to cover this service and subsequently to operate its expanding network. As a result, between 1864 and 1870 the Met commissioned the construction of 44 Class A 4-4-0 tanks, followed by 22 of an improved version (Class B). The District, which commenced operations shortly after the Met, initially under a joint-working agreement with the Met for the operation of what later became the Circle Line, purchased 54 very similar locomotives.

In the 1900s the electrification of both the Met, as far as Harrow-on-the-Hill, and the District, rendered the elderly Met Class A and B tanks, together with their equivalents on the District, largely superfluous and most were sold or scrapped. The Met still needed steam locomotives for the main-line services beyond Harrow from 1908 (beyond Rickmansworth from 1925, following further electrification) to its outpost at Verney Junction, near Winslow in Buckinghamshire. The Class E tanks were used on these services until replaced by more powerful locomotives obtained between 1916 and 1925, whereupon the remaining Class E tanks were given lighter duties, including the working of the Chesham branch until 1937.

Towards the end of the 19th century the Met was associated with some unusual, albeit unsuccessful schemes through the inspiration of its visionary Chairman, Sir Edward Watkin. Controlling several railway companies, Watkin had an ambitious scheme for a main line under single management from the Midlands to France via a Channel tunnel, but the scheme failed after only two miles of tunnel had been built, due largely to public concern about its potential use by foreign invaders. To attract more business to the Met, Watkin had also proposed a taller version of the Eiffel Tower on what was to become the site of Wembley Stadium, but this scheme was aborted when the tower had reached only 155ft in height, by which time it had already been nicknamed 'Watkin's Folly'. The Met also had more modest ambitions, such as extending the Quainton Road–Brill branch (closed in 1935) to Oxford and the Chesham branch to Tring, but these plans similarly never came to fruition.

Verney Junction was as far north as the Met reached. Indeed, this station, on the Oxford–Cambridge line (today a candidate for reopening as part of the East–West Rail Link) and the line to Buckingham and Banbury, was situated in the middle of nowhere, being named, in the absence of any significant settlement, after the local landowner. Inherited by LT in 1933, it was regarded as too remote from the capital to justify a service, and as a result the line was cut back to Aylesbury in 1936. The following year the 18 larger Met locomotives were sold to the London & North Eastern Railway (LNER), which assumed responsibility for providing the motive power beyond Rickmansworth on the through passenger trains from Baker Street/Liverpool Street/Aldgate to Aylesbury and on the Chesham branch. Upon nationalisation in 1948 responsibility passed to the Eastern Region (ER) of British Railways, and subsequently to the London Midland Region (LMR). Finally the Met was cut back from Aylesbury to Amersham in 1961, coinciding with the much-delayed electrification of the main line beyond Rickmansworth. So ended scheduled steam-operated passenger services on LT, although steam continued for a further 10 years on freight/engineering trains and shunting operations.

Living near Ealing Broadway, served by the District and Central lines, I developed a keen interest in the Underground and was fascinated by the strange and archaic Met services out of Baker Street. Indeed, in my early teens I travelled with a friend on the special train marking the end of scheduled steam operations, on 9 September 1961. I still have the ticket to prove it (reproduced below), duly signed by the engine crew, and the commemorative scroll with opening dates for the various sections of line between Baker Street and Amersham. The same date saw the transfer from LT to BR of stations beyond Amersham, these being Great Missenden, Wendover, Stoke Mandeville and Aylesbury. All are still open, unlike the former LT stations beyond Aylesbury — Waddesdon, Quainton Road, Grandborough Road, Winslow Road, Verney Junction and, on the branch from Quainton Road, Waddesdon Road, Westcott, Wotton, Wood Siding (arguably the most unlikely-sounding abandoned Underground station!) and Brill.

Since 1961 steam has reappeared from time to time on special passenger workings, notably the wonderful Steam on the Met specials, but the last occasion was some years ago, and it now looks, sadly, as though steam on the Underground has gone for good.

For this album I have sourced information from the many publications about the Underground which have been produced over the years, and I should like to mention, in particular, the excellent book entitled *Red Panniers* (Lightmoor Press, 2008) by John Scott-Morgan and Kirk Martin. I should also like to thank the photographers who have very kindly provided their precious material — Michael Allen, Nick Lera, Bruce Jenkins, Roy Hobbs, Peter Zabek, David Clark, Jim Oatway and Neil Davenport. Photographs by Harry Luff, Marcus Eavis, Ray DeGroote, E. J. McWatt and Ron Copson are reproduced courtesy of the Online Transport Archive, those by Frank Hunt courtesy of the Light Rail Transit Association (London Branch) and by Ken Wightman courtesy of David Clark.

For convenience, the pictures in the main body of this book have been sorted into the following sequential batches, starting with the last steam-hauled passenger trains (*i.e.* those operating beyond Rickmansworth, including the Chesham branch and the 1963 Centenary special), then ex-Met locomotives on railtours, the Underground Centenary celebrations, Epping–Ongar services, freight/engineering trains (including the Watford/Croxley rubbish-tip operations), depot scenes and adjacent operations and ending with the farewell steam-hauled engineering-train special.

Kevin R. McCormack
Ashtead, Surrey
December 2010

Right: Notice announcing the end of LT steam between Aylesbury and Rickmansworth on 9 September 1961. *Michael Allen*

Far right: In this view at Rickmansworth on the last day the electric locomotive has been detached from the 8.34am Liverpool Street–Aylesbury service to enable Fairburn 2-6-4 tank No 42253 to be coupled to the train. The latter's home depot was Aylesbury, a sub-shed of Neasden. *Michael Allen*

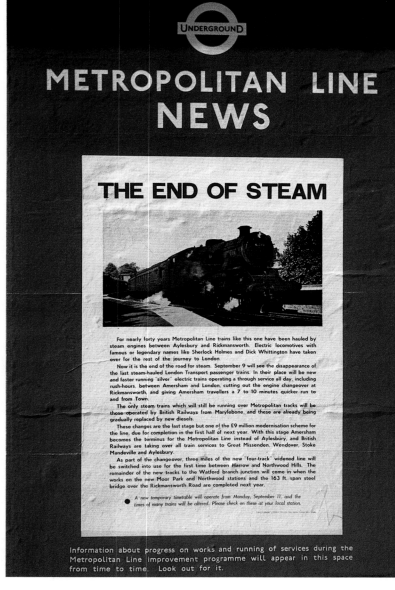

UNDERGROUND

METROPOLITAN LINE NEWS

THE END OF STEAM

For nearly forty years Metropolitan Line trains like this one have been hauled by steam engines between Aylesbury and Rickmansworth. Electric locomotives with famous or legendary names like Sherlock Holmes and Dick Whittington have taken over for the rest of the journey to London.

Now it is the end of the road for steam. September 9 will see the disappearance of the last steam-hauled London Transport passenger trains. In their place will be new and faster running "silver" electric trains operating a through service all day, including rush-hours, between Amersham and London, cutting out the engine changeover at Rickmansworth, and giving Amersham travellers a 7 to 10 minutes quicker run to and from Town.

The only steam trains which will still be running over Metropolitan tracks will be those operated by British Railways from Marylebone, and these are already being gradually replaced by new diesels.

These changes are the last stage but one of the £9 million modernisation scheme for the line, due for completion in the first half of next year. With this stage Amersham becomes the terminus for the Metropolitan Line instead of Aylesbury, and British Railways are taking over all train services to Great Missenden, Wendover, Stoke Mandeville and Aylesbury.

As part of the changeover, three miles of the new "four-track" widened line will be switched into use for the first time between Harrow and Northwood Hills. The remainder of the new tracks to the Watford branch junction will come in when the works on the new Moor Park and Northwood stations and the 163 ft. span steel bridge over the Rickmansworth Road are completed next year.

● A new temporary timetable will operate from Monday, September 11, and the times of many trains will be altered. Please check on these at your local station.

Information about progress on works and running of services during the Metropolitan Line improvement programme will appear in this space from time to time. Look out for it.

Left: Another photograph taken on 9 September 1961, as Fairburn Class 4MT 2-6-4 tank No 42281 brings the 9.15am Aylesbury–Baker Street into Chorley Wood. Steam locomotives — LT's own and those of BR working LT trains — operated with smokebox facing London. *Michael Allen*

Above: Used on the Chesham branch were two three-car sets of former electric stock (built as steam stock and subsequently converted back) dating from the period 1898-1900, of which five carriages survive (four on the Bluebell Railway and one in the LT Museum). Ivatt Class 2 No 41284 hauls a set into Chalfont & Latimer in the summer of 1960. *Marcus Eavis / Online Transport Archive*

NOTICE

PASSENGERS MUST NOT ATTEMPT TO
ENTER OR LEAVE CARS BEYOND THIS
POINT, NOR CROSS THE LINE EXCEPT
BY THE BRIDGE OR SUBWAY PROVIDED.

WARNING TO STAFF
DO NOT STEP ON ANY RAIL

Left: On 27 March 1954, when the ER still had responsibility for providing passenger motive power for LT trains north of Rickmansworth, Class L1 2-6-4 tank No 67789 enters Chalfont & Latimer from Aylesbury. These locomotives were also used at this time on BR trains between Aylesbury and Marylebone, which shared the Met tracks at this point, but the red-painted carriage end identifies this as an LT train. *Neil Davenport*

Above: The conductor rails are already in place for the imminent electrification of the Chesham branch in this view of Ivatt '2MT' No 41272 approaching Chalfont & Latimer in the summer of 1960. The branch opened in 1889, three years before Amersham was reached, Chesham therefore serving briefly as the Met's northern terminus. *Bruce Jenkins*

In 1937 the LNER assumed responsibility for providing locomotives for passenger trains on the remaining non-electrified section of the Met (*i.e.* beyond Rickmansworth), and shortly afterwards ex-Great Central Railway Class C13 4-4-2 tanks became the regular motive power for the Chesham branch, lasting until 1957/8. In this and the following view 'C13' No 67418 is pictured at Chesham in 1954. *Frank Hunt / Light Rail Transit Association*

In the early 1950s brown paint began to replace the varnished teak finish of the Met's coaching stock, although it was 1957 before the Chesham sets were so treated. These vehicles were the last survivors of the so-called 'Bogie' stock built by the Ashbury Railway Carriage & Iron Co for the steam-hauled main-line services, the fleet having been converted into electric units between 1906 and 1924 as electrification of the Met spread. *Frank Hunt / Light Rail Transit Association*

Above: In this view from 1961, Fairburn tank No 42082 is leaving Amersham for Rickmansworth with a rake of 'Dreadnoughts'. These carriages replaced the 'Bogie' stock, which was regarded as inferior to the Great Central's more modern suburban stock used on the rival service from Marylebone. The 'Dreadnought' fleet totalled 92 vehicles built between 1910 and 1923, the first 10 being rebuilds of 1905 stock. Three carriages used on the Centenary special (see opposite) have been preserved on the Keighley & Worth Valley Railway. *Marcus Eavis / Online Transport Archive*

Right: On 26 May 1963, to commemorate the Underground's Centenary, one final train ran from Baker Street to Aylesbury, steam taking over from electric traction at Amersham. For the special day BR produced an interesting express passenger locomotive, 'Jubilee' No 45709 *Implacable*, although its lined green livery was concealed beneath a layer of grime. The train is seen leaving Amersham for Aylesbury, with Met electric locomotive No 5 *John Hampden* in the background. *Michael Allen*

Above: Fairburn 2-6-4 tank No 42089 arrives at Amersham with the 12.33pm Liverpool Street–Aylesbury on 1 July 1961. The first 'Dreadnought' coach in the formation, although not electric stock, was always fitted with collector shoes in order to assist electric locomotives, which, owing to their relatively short length, might otherwise lose traction over points at major junctions. The shoes were normally fitted to just one side of the carriage (the down side, *i.e.* outward from London).
Michael Allen

Right: Another view of Amersham on 1 July 1961 with Fairburn No 42251 arriving with the 1.18pm Aylesbury–Baker Street.
Michael Allen

Above: 'Jubilee' No 45709 *Implacable* brings the Underground Centenary special through Great Missenden on 26 May 1963 on its return from Aylesbury to Baker Street. Given the tremendous effort LT put into marking the Centenary, it is extraordinary that BR should have provided a locomotive in such outwardly appalling condition, although, in terms of a re-enactment of the final years up to 1961, it was at least providing an authentic representation of the normal condition of the LMR's tank engines. *Michael Allen*

Right: It's back to the last day, 9 September 1961, for this view of Fairburn tank No 42230 at Wendover, working the 12.05pm Aylesbury–Liverpool Street service. In preparation for the imminent takeover by BR of all workings to/from this station the LT nameboards have been covered over with temporary BR(LMR) totem signs. *Michael Allen*

Left: The practice of painting the ends of brake stock red began in 1953 at the request of LT staff, to make the vehicles more visible at night and so facilitate coupling and uncoupling. The round tops to the doors were intended to minimise damage if one were opened in a tunnel. This last-day image depicts the 11.15am from Baker Street to Aylesbury at Wendover. *Michael Allen*

Above: Fairburn '4MT' No 42070 was the locomotive that hauled the special farewell train over the steam-operated section of line on the last day. It is seen here at Stoke Mandeville a few days earlier, by which time a start had been made on making it look respectable. Maintenance for the joint BR/LT section was shared on the basis of alternating five-year terms, and LT appears to have fitted new platform-edging stones (they are of LT pattern) to this station very recently, despite the fact that it is about to be handed over to BR. *Marcus Eavis / Online Transport Archive*

The 12.56pm from Liverpool Street has just arrived at Aylesbury on 1 July 1961, hauled by '4MT' No 42159. This station was officially named Aylesbury Town because there was already a separate, and much older, Aylesbury station (latterly called Aylesbury High Street) which was the terminus of a branch from Cheddington on the LNWR's main line out of Euston, this branch closing to passengers in 1950 and to freight in 1963. *Michael Allen*

Above: By way of a change, this BR locomotive, No 42618, is not one of the usual Fairburn tanks (which were postwar machines) but a prewar Stanier engine. It is seen at Aylesbury in 1959 at the head of a London-bound Met train. Fowler Class 4 tanks were also used occasionally in the 1950s (see page 38 of the author's earlier book, *The Midland around London*). *Marcus Eavis / Online Transport Archive*

Left: Although normal services were still operating to Aylesbury on 9 September 1961, the farewell special ran only as far as Amersham. This was also the last day for Ladies Only compartments on LT; thereafter female passengers would have to tolerate the company of men, for the replacement 'A60' stock, like other Underground electric units, was open-plan. *Michael Allen*

Above and right: On 23 May 1954 a railtour operated between Moorgate and Quainton Road, hauled by the penultimate of seven Class E 0-4-4 tanks, No L48 (ex Met No 81). By this time there was no evidence of the condensing apparatus which had originally been fitted to this class for working through tunnels. The special is seen at Willesden Green on its outward journey. *Frank Hunt / Light Rail Transit Association*

Left: Whereas the last four Class E tanks were built by Hawthorn Leslie in 1900/1, the first three had been built at Neasden works in the years 1896-8, among them No L46 (ex Met No 77, the pioneer, built in 1896). It is pictured at Hammersmith on 22 September 1957, waiting to replace an electric locomotive on a Stephenson Locomotive Society railtour over the Hammersmith & City and Inner Circle lines. The special started at Edgware Road and terminated at Wembley Park. *Bruce Jenkins*

Above: Although there were just seven Class E tanks, a gap in the Met's numbering system suggests that as many as seven further examples of this small passenger type may have been envisaged. However, the order appears to have been abandoned due to the spread of electrification and to the heavier loads being carried on the remaining steam-operated section of the main line. No L44 (ex Met No 1), the last of the Neasden-built trio, is seen at New Cross Gate on 1 October 1961 working a railtour over the East London line and the Stanmore branch. *Bruce Jenkins*

Above: Forget that this is the railtour seen on the previous page on its approach to Stanmore; add another carriage, and No L44 could easily be deputising for a failed BR locomotive between Rickmansworth and Aylesbury, for which eventuality a Class E 0-4-4T was for some years stationed at Rickmansworth. *Roy Hobbs*

Inset: Substituting for a BR locomotive, No 44 reaches Dutchlands Summit with an Aylesbury–Baker Street on 12 August 1951. *L. J. Dew*

Right: Surrounded by 1938 Tube stock, each set lengthened by the addition of a trailer from 1927 stock, No L44 runs round its train at Stanmore on 1 October 1961. The Stanmore branch from Wembley Park was the Met's final expansionist act prior to absorption by LT and opened in December 1932, with electric traction from the outset. Transferred from the Met to the Bakerloo in 1939, the branch now forms part of the Jubilee Line. *Roy Hobbs*

Above: In this and the next view No L44 has just arrived at Stanmore with its railtour on 1 October 1961. This locomotive, which (along with pannier tank No L99) now resides at the Buckinghamshire Railway Centre at Quainton Road, has led a charmed life, largely on account of its former identity as Met No 1 (whereas logically it probably should have been No 79). Completed in 1898, it replaced the original No 1, Class A *Jupiter*, withdrawn following an accident at Baker Street (although this engine is understood to have been used subsequently as a stationary boiler at Wembley Park to generate current for electrification experiments). *Bruce Jenkins*

Right: Hauling specials has been a feature of No L44's life. Due to a six-month delay in completion of electrification, trains on the Uxbridge branch were initially steam-hauled, and as Met No 1 this locomotive was chosen to haul the inaugural train in June 1904, for which occasion it was extravagantly decorated. In the summer of 2007 it visited the Bluebell Railway in East Sussex and made a fine sight hauling the four restored Chesham carriages. *Marcus Eavis / Online Transport Archive*

LT celebrated the centenary of the worlds oldest underground railway system in impressive style from 23 to 26 May 1963, deciding to defer the event from the actual centenary date in January in anticipation of inclement weather — a wise move, considering that it would have coincided with the severest winter experienced in London since 1947!

On 24 May — 101 years to the day since the first section of line was inspected by various VIPs — a re-enactment using No L48 was held on Platform 5 at Moorgate for the benefit of the Lord Mayor of London and other dignitaries — not to mention local office workers! *Roy Hobbs*

No L48 brings the wagons representing the 1862 inspection train up to the buffers at Platform 5. Observant readers may spot a second locomotive at the rear of the train; this was L44, which, coupled to a brake van, removed the wagons once the tableau had finished (see front cover). Both locomotives were lucky to survive into the 1960s; three of the class of seven had been withdrawn as early as 1935, without even being renumbered in the 'L' series. *Roy Hobbs*

Above: Built in 1866, Met Class A No 23 was another locomotive to lead a charmed life. Following electrification of the sub-surface lines in 1905 (for which purpose it had been fitted with condensing apparatus to reduce smoke emissions in tunnels) it was retained for miscellaneous duties and, along with another member of the class, was later used on the Brill branch. After closure of the branch in 1935 it became the sole survivor and, renumbered L45, was retained for freight work until withdrawn for preservation in 1948. No longer in working order, this veteran took part in the Centenary Parade at Neasden on 23 May 1963, with power provided by a battery locomotive. It now resides in the LT Museum at Covent Garden. *Nick Lera*

Right: A dress rehearsal (literally, in the case of the members of the LT Musical & Dramatic Society seen here!) for the centenary celebrations took place at Neasden on 19 May 1963. As depicted in the previous picture, Met No 23 was attached to two LT wagons adapted to resemble the trucks of Smith & Knight (builder of the Paddington–Gower Street section of the original line), in which the distinguished party — including Prime Minister William Gladstone and his wife — had travelled on 24 May 1862 to inspect the work in progress. *Bruce Jenkins*

Above: Besides Met No 23 there were three working steam locomotives hauling demonstration trains in the Centenary Parade of 23 May 1963. Class F No L52 hauled a works train, pannier No L98 hauled a cable-laying train, and, as seen here at the dress rehearsal on 19 May 1963, No L44 hauled restored Met milk van No 3 (formerly tool van No 700) and the Chesham carriages borrowed from the Bluebell Railway. *Bruce Jenkins*

Right: On the weekend of 25/26 May a static display of locomotives and rolling stock was held at Neasden, although the 'Dreadnought' carriages were absent on the Sunday, being used for the special train to Aylesbury hauled by Met electric locomotive No 5 and BR 'Jubilee' No 45709. In this busy scene on the Saturday, illustrating the popularity of the event, Met electric locomotive No 1 *John Lyon* (surprisingly rejected for static preservation in favour of No 5) is at the head of the 'Dreadnought' set, standing alongside No L44. *Michael Allen*

Met Class F consisted of four 0-6-2 tanks built in 1901 by the Yorkshire Engine Co and designed primarily for freight work. No L52 was the last survivor and was initially earmarked for preservation by LT but was ultimately rejected on account of a cracked frame. The locomotive is pictured experiencing its penultimate day of glory as part of the Centenary display at Neasden on 25 May 1963. *Michael Allen*

A Central Line train from Ongar arrives at Epping c1957 behind ex-Great Eastern Railway Class M15 (LNER Class F5) 2-4-2 tank No 67200. Thirty-two 'M15s', constructed between 1884 and 1909, were rebuilt between 1911 and 1920 with higher-pressure boilers, among them this example, one of seven fitted for push-pull working from 1949. As no GER 2-4-2s survive, the Holden F5 Locomotive Trust has been formed to construct a replica locomotive to run on the now preserved Epping–Ongar line. *Frank Hunt / Light Rail Transit Association*

Left: The steam/electric interchange at Epping, pictured on 28 May 1955. Epping, Ongar and the intermediate stations at Blake Hall and North Weald were opened by the GER on 24 April 1865 and became part of the London Underground on 25 September 1949 following the postwar extension of the Central Line eastward from Liverpool Street to Epping. However, electrification was not extended to Ongar until 18 November 1957, so for more than eight years LT 'hired' a steam-powered push-pull shuttle from BR. *Ray DeGroote / Online Transport Archive*

Above: Class F5 No 67200 stands at Ongar station on 28 May 1955. Despite subsequent electrification, passenger numbers on the Epping–Ongar section declined, resulting in the closure of Blake Hall station on 31 October 1981 and complete closure of the line on 30 September 1994. The railway is now in private hands, with diesel trains operating periodically since 2004 between Ongar and North Weald, but is currently closed while works are carried out to allow a resumption of steam working. *Ray DeGroote / Online Transport Archive*

Left and above: Apart from Class E 0-4-4s covering for the occasional LNER/BR locomotive failure and operating railtours, from 1937 LT steam was confined to non-passenger duties, *i.e.* engineering or freight trains — and yard shunting — on surface and sub-surface lines across the Underground network. These pictures taken on 29 May 1955 depict Class E No L46 at Rayners Lane and ex-District Railway Hunslet 0-6-0 No L30 at Farringdon. *Ray DeGroote / Online Transport Archive (both)*

Left and right: Ex-GWR pannier tanks ultimately replaced all the former Met/District steam locomotives, being introduced following acquisition by LT between October 1956 and August 1963. The first two, Nos L90 and L91, were substituted by a new L90 and L91 when they required heavy repairs, the original L90 being returned to BR in September 1961. The first view shows this locomotive rounding the curve into Farringdon station from Barbican on the Met/Circle Line, while the second photograph depicts No L97 approaching Farringdon on 27 January 1968 from the opposite direction and crossing over to LT's Widened Lines, over which BR trains travelled to Barbican and Moorgate.
Harry Luff / Online Transport Archive; Peter Zabek

Left: Because of the track layout, trains leaving the District's Lillie Bridge engineering depot near Earl's Court and travelling westwards towards Baron's Court had to join the eastbound District Line at West Kensington station. In this view locomotive No L94 (built by the North British Locomotive Co in 1930), coupled to one of six brake vans built at BR's Ashford Works in 1962, hurries to the crossover in order to cease this wrong-line working. *E. J. McWatt / Online Transport Archive*

Above: The first of a sequence of photographs featuring No L94 on an LT/BR transfer working in August 1970. Here, having passed above the District Line near Lillie Bridge / West Kensington station and under the West Cromwell Road, the locomotive is travelling along the LT track leading to Kensington Olympia with two empty wagons and a brake van built in 1935 by Hurst Nelson, of Motherwell. *Harry Luff / Online Transport Archive*

Above: With the Olympia Exhibition Hall and 'Official Garage' visible behind, No L94 has now crossed over to BR metals to reach the exchange sidings and detaches the brake van carrying the LT guard (furthest from the camera) and the BR pilot guard. *Harry Luff / Online Transport Archive*

Right: Having deposited the trucks, No L94 runs forward to collect the brake van and return to Lillie Bridge depot. The building on the left was originally home to William Whiteley's Furniture Depositories, belonging to the famous Bayswater department store, while in the background is the National Savings Bank complex in Kensington High Street. *Harry Luff / Online Transport Archive*

Above: In January 1961 ex-District Railway Hunslet 0-6-0 No L31 heads east from Acton Town with a freight composed of BR wagons. The wagons, to be handed over to BR at Kensington, may have come from South Harrow Gasworks, although the first three could have been collected from Acton Underground Works. *Colour-Rail (LT 237)*

Right: Major overhauls of the pannier tanks were carried out under contract by BR, initially at Swindon and latterly at Eastleigh. On its way for overhaul in the spring of 1965, No L94 arrives 'on shed' at Southall, enabling the locomotive to fraternise with old comrades. Restricted tunnel clearances caused LT to purchase the older 'flat-roofed' pannier tanks (and even these had to have minor modifications made) rather than more modern panniers with larger cabs, such as the one behind. *Author*

Due to their random nature or nightime operation, steam-worked freight/engineering trains were seldom photographed, an exception being the regular daytime waste train from Neasden to Croxley Tip, near Watford. In the first of a series of views of this train recorded on separate occasions No L94 is seen just north of Pinner station on 28 December 1967 with loaded wagons for the tip. *Peter Zabek*

On 30 June 1969 a group of workmen stop to watch No L89 as it brings loaded wagons for the tip through Croxley station, on the Met's Watford branch (opened 1925). They may be surprised a little later to see the same train travelling in the opposite direction, still heading for the tip! *David Clark*

The mystery explained. Access to the tip was from the Watford direction, so the train, with the locomotive normally travelling bunker-first from Neasden, went past the tip entrance and onwards to Watford (Met). Here it entered a loop, where the locomotive would run round its train (hence the brake vans at each end), taking water at the station platform in the process, and would then proceed smokebox-first to the tip. This photograph, also featuring No L89, was taken in September 1968. *Harry Luff / Online Transport Archive*

Another view at Watford (Met) in September 1968 depicting No L89, which along with No L98 had apparently suffered corrosion to its panniers (water tanks) and consequently had the lower part reinforced.

The locomotive is seen waiting to cross over to the station, having uncoupled from its train, in order to take water. *Harry Luff / Online Transport Archive*

Above: No L89 takes water from the column (now preserved at the Buckinghamshire Railway Centre at Quainton Road) at Watford (Met) station while a train of 'A60' electric stock waits in the siding. *Harry Luff / Online Transport Archive*

Right: Having reattached itself to the waste train, but at the opposite end, the second No L91 (minus top-feed) heads out of Watford (Met) for Croxley Tip on 4 December 1967. *Peter Zabek*

Above: The Croxley Tip waste train approaching Croxley station on 4 July 1969, this time from the Watford rather than the Neasden direction, with No L92 in charge. The leading brake van is one of the BR Ashford-built examples dating from 1962, while the second dates from 1935 and was constructed by Hurst Nelson. *David Clark*

Right: On 1 December 1968, having passed through Croxley station, No L89 approaches Watford South Junction, where the Watford branch and Met mainline split. Branching off immediately before this point is the line into the Croxley Tip sidings. *Peter Zabek*

Above and right: In these snowy scenes, recorded on 11 January 1968, the second No L90 is pictured first in the sidings, pushing the loaded wagons towards the tip, and then, having deposited these wagons, propelling a train of empty trucks out onto the Watford branch before returning them to Neasden. The locomotive's diamond-shaped North British Locomotive Co builder's plate is visible on the front splasher. *Peter Zabek (both)*

Left: Heavy snow arrived in London on Boxing Day 1962 and stayed for more than a month. The results of the ensuing clearance operations at Moor Park are evident in this photograph, taken on 11 January 1963, of No L96 hauling a rake of empty wagons. The locomotive carries its LT motif higher up the tank sides than on most other panniers and is also minus its top-feed apparatus. *Bruce Jenkins*

Below left: In considerably better weather conditions No L92 is seen near Pinner Green on 4 July 1969, returning to Neasden from Croxley Tip with its train of empties, comprising two flat wagons and one rail wagon, plus the obligatory pair of brake vans. The tip train ran daily from Monday to Friday, and around this time there was a large amount of debris to be carried, due to the demolition of the power station at Neasden. *David Clark*

Right: Returning from Croxley, the original No L90 (ex GWR No 7711) draws into Harrow-on-the-Hill station in February 1961, its train comprising wagons containing wood (probably for lighting locomotive fires) and a steam crane from the tip, presumably bound for Neasden for maintenance or repair. The last steam-hauled Croxley Tip working ran on 18 May 1971, with No L94 in charge. *Bruce Jenkins*

Although Neasden was the Underground's principal steam shed, a few locomotives were outstationed at the District's Lillie Bridge engineering depot, near Earl's Court. This had been the home of the last of the District's original Beyer Peacock 4-4-0 tanks and an almost identical one bought from the Met in 1925, which worked there until the arrival in 1931 of two Hunslet 0-6-0 tanks. These became Nos L30 and L31, the latter being seen outside the locomotive shed in 1961. Both would be withdrawn in 1963 upon replacement by pannier tanks. *Jim Oatway*

For shunting at Neasden and Finchley Road the Met purchased two Peckett saddle tanks, in 1897 and 1899, which survived until 1960 and 1961 respectively. The later example, No L54 (ex Met No 102), is seen assembling a works train at Lillie Bridge in April 1958. *Bruce Jenkins*

Above and right: Lillie Bridge depot early in 1969, with pannier No L92 shunting alongside the Stores building. Visible in the first view are the Goliath crane, the locomotive shed (with ventilators on the roof) and the bridge supporting West Cromwell Road. *Author (both)*

Above: No L94 stands at the coaling stage outside Lillie Bridge locomotive shed in August 1970. The tracks nearest the shed give access to West Kensington station and to the erstwhile West London Extension Railway leading to Kensington Olympia (formerly Addison Road). Brackets for train-reporting numbers were fitted to LT panniers fairly late in their career, the numbers being displayed approximately where their brackets for their BR smokebox numberplates had been affixed. *Harry Luff / Online Transport Archive*

Right: In February 1971, four months before being given the honour of hauling the commemorative last steam train on the Underground, No L94 visited Ealing Common depot for overhaul. In this view the locomotive is supported by hydraulic jacks, enabling its wheels to be removed. *Harry Luff / Online Transport Archive*

Above: Viewed from a passing train, Class E 0-4-4 tank No L48 stands at the northern end of Neasden shed in the summer of 1962. The splendid building in the background is Neasden power station, built in 1904 for the Met electrification and closed in 1968. *Neil Davenport*

Right: The shed at Neasden replaced a bigger structure following the transfer of the larger locomotives to the LNER in 1937. This view, dating from the late 1960s, features the second No L90 (left) and No L99 (right), the latter identifiable by the rows of rivets on its tanks. This feature distinguished the only two Kerr Stuart-built locomotives (the other being the first No L90, by now withdrawn) from the rest of the LT pannier fleet. *E. J. McWatt / Online Transport Archive*

The first ex-GWR pannier tank was the original No L90, which was purchased in October 1956 following successful trials (which began in February of that year) and replaced Class F 0-6-2 No L51. The only LT pannier not to have its BR smokebox-numberplate brackets removed, it is seen shunting in Neasden's top sidings in 1957. Note that the fence is being supported by a combination of old railway sleepers and short lengths of rail! *Harry Luff / Online Transport Archive*

Shortly before withdrawal in September 1957 and replacement by pannier No L91, Class F 0-6-2 No L49 stands in the top sidings at Neasden. Dating from 1901 and originally Met No 90, this locomotive was the first of four designed for freight work and built by the Yorkshire Engine Co. *Harry Luff / Online Transport Archive*

Above and right: Two photographs taken at Neasden shed on 4 November 1961. The first depicts the second No L91 (ex GWR No 5757), supplied as a replacement for the original (classmate No 5752), which, having been sent to Swindon for overhaul in November 1960, was found to require extensive repairs and as a result became the first LT pannier to be withdrawn. The second view features Class E 0-4-4 No L48 (ex Met No 81), from the batch of four built by Hawthorn Leslie in 1900/1. *Michael Allen (both)*

The second No L90, built by the North British Locomotive Co in 1931 and acquired by LT in November 1961, shunts at Neasden soon after its purchase. In the background can be seen Met 'A60' and 1938 Tube stock, as well as the twin chimneys of Neasden power station.

The panniers needed little modification to work on LT — essentially just minor alterations to the cab roof and the fitting of the trip-cock (train-protection) mechanism. *Harry Luff / Online Transport Archive*

Left: No L93 (ex No 7739, built by Armstrong Whitworth in 1930) passed to LT in November 1958. Photographed in the early 1960s it still retained its vacuum-brake and steam-heating equipment — fittings no longer required, as the panniers were not intended for working passenger trains. *R. Copson / Online Transport Archive*

Above: The second No L90 marshals a ballast train in the top sidings at Neasden in early 1970. Hanging from the cab are the curtains which were fitted in an attempt to reduce the amount of smoke inhaled by engine crew in tunnels. The 11 pannier tanks fitted with condensing apparatus for working over Met lines to the GWR's Smithfield goods depot might have been preferred by LT, but their larger cabs would have ruled them out. *Harry Luff / Online Transport Archive*

Replaced by a trio of second-hand diesel locomotives, the last three panniers — Nos L90, L94 and L95 — were withdrawn in June 1971. The culmination of 108 years of steam operation by LT and its predecessors was marked on 6 June 1971 by the running of a ceremonial engineering train from Moorgate to Neasden, where an open day was held. No L94, the last LT locomotive to be overhauled, had the honour of hauling the special and is seen leaving Farringdon in the presence of a few spectators! *Author's collection*